CW01023269

AFTER 8 BOOKS ☺

⌂ 7 RUE JARRY
75010 PARIS X

WWW.AFTER8BOOKS.COM

⌂ 09 72936159 ☎

"FEELINGS ARE FACTS, OR BOOKS"

CUNT-UPS

CUNT-UPS
DODIE BELLAMY

TENDER BUTTONS

New York City

2018

Copyright © 2001 by Dodie Bellamy
17th Anniversary Edition 2018
All rights reserved to the author

Tender Buttons Press
Lee Ann Brown, Founding Editrix
New York, New York
www.TenderButtonsPress.com

Book design: Wayne Smith
Cover art: *Hedgehog Touching Herself*, Michelle Rollman, 2000
Inside art: *Hedgehog Touching Herself Some More*, Michelle Rollman, 2017
Tender Buttons logo by Joe Brainard, printed with permission
Special thanks to Tender Buttons' Star Arkestress, Katy Bohinc

ISBN 978-0-927920-179

FOREWORD: DESIRE'S WIDE HIGHWAY
SOPHIE ROBINSON

Cunt-Ups consists of a series of 21 pornographic chapters,
described by Bellamy as "a hermaphroditic salute to William
Burroughs and Kathy Acker." The result is a kind of subjectless
and objectless pornography that defies the limits of sex, genre,
narrative, and time. It's cooler than porn, and more radical; a
sexual universe in which everything is perverted by the random
violence of desire and writing.

One obvious effect of Bellamy's use of Burroughs' cut-up
technique is the incongruence of temporalities, grammars,
genres and genders throughout the text. We're always being
relocated. Subjects disintegrate, become disembodied parts: "my
teeth stuck out like separate vampires and each touched you."
Cunts become clouds, cocks become butterflies. Sex is not an
action but a mood, a filter over the landscape. It's everything
that's happening. Bellamy's pornographic source material acts
as a kind of erotic Midas touch, making all it brushes up against
sexy and queer. In this text sex is immanent; it is what pulses
and writhes in an eternal present that forgets itself.

Cunt-Ups also challenges what vocabularies are appropriate
or fun for the expression of sexual desire. Bellamy highlights
the limitations placed on language within the genre of porn,

opening the curtain on what these limitations conceal of the connection between sex and other ways of being, of feeling. Bellamy's inclusion of Jeffrey Dahmer's confessions as a source text, alongside zombies, the nautical, the bucolic and the technological raise the question of the limits of desire within genre, and the ways in which genre and gender shape each other. The soft eroticism of the bucolic body in nature gives way to the cock and tits of porn, then to dead flesh, to networks, to circuitry, to sea and sky. We're queer and we want it weirder: by expanding the genre of pornography by shooting it through with languages from other parts of the universe, Bellamy exposes the banality and repetition of the language or pornographic titilation. This is porn unbound, a blasphemous and spiritual expansion of what's hot, a celestial cumshot. Everybody who's ever had the good sex knows it took them places.

The queer temporality of this book is in its constant revision of the moment and hand, rather than a linearity of past, present and future. The text is made of 21 pages spliced together and reworked into 21 parts, but, from the process and the source materials, hundreds of variations of the same text could have been produced. There's an ephemerality and contingency to *Cunt-Ups*, amplified by shifts in tones and tenses as well as contexts and vocabularies. Repetitions and echoes amass (cock appears 110 times, fuck and cunt appear 50 times each, and honourable mentions go to nipple, ass and pussy) and these repetitions function as a beat, "keeping" time, a pulse of desire, reminding us why we're here. *Cunt-Ups* exists in a queer spacetime in which we oscillate between remembering and forgetting, between the past and the future, between copy and original, and it is precisely the quest of this small, kinky, strange and beautiful book to never let the dust settle, to keep us moving along desire's wide highway to nowhere.

FOR KEVIN

screens flicker

with pornography, with science-ficton vampires

—ADRIENNE RICH

"Twenty-One Love Poems"

ONE

Without its shell, but it's tubular, like most and I was raised there and attended and we fall asleep together. I'll wake up when you pinch my nipple, I'll look back at you when you tell me to rub cum juice on my living. Will you accept my pussy for your subject states? I was raised—think of it as yours. Would you do it? I consider myself to be an atheist, I admit I pussy weep. Would you feel okay about states? I am currently on probation for thoughts mushy and oozing like runny yolks, thoughts about age and ass. Would you prefer me to suck your clit, hiker, whom I described as a male with lips? Yes, I would fuck you back, yes, you had homosexual sex with me and states sexy. You are such a romantic. You can state we got into a physical fight, you can hang there with my balls, you can, and during the fight you stated your cock could slide up anything you want *blow of the* *barbell* 'cause you can't help it now, it's magic, you've got to blur, I'm moving so fast. You don't know how infinite the course of my humiliations for you, singing actually—torch songs of nullity of being/being outside my kind of love, the kind of love the top of the wall carved a hole in. The rock. They opened the door, and tied me down, a runnel of water/a returned letter. They tied me down, and I let a turd, the hard absolute hostility of slaves, the infinite partition of waiting because my eyes were too wide. I was Jesus, see the dark figure in the empty room alone, all fours tied, cakes, one arm out of the leather. Then I got a foot out and I couldn't decide whether I had turned in the electric symbols. I knew you were there outside in black black black cell of rock. What else do you want to know about me *the rock well walls of rock* I'm yours. Chinks of light. When I was in SF I again thought I was your wall of light, UFOs set up a landing near the wailing wall, cement pads. I painted pictures because I reached the hall of the Double Rhino, I walked around a government building, ripped leaves from the trees and wrote down that I had so many choices.

TWO

Breasts, but I couldn't find your nipples. I'll fuck you like I've never fucked, a bit funky, I felt you biting the insides of my cunt and you heave, and inside my cunt you would have seen lime too. And I'll suck your cock too, I won't forget having been slapped to your pillows, and I've only been fucked in the ass. Subject states like two halves of a movement, slightly, just slightly, slower touching that little space between my clit. And so I fuck you until you scream creamy, the only table in the world, I'm there, bang your cock against the back of my throat FAITH you left my open insides and went to fill yourself and tried to hold onto it. And then we did get arrested. You thought maybe I'd give myself to you in ways I'd never given myself when taking polaroid pictures. I fucked you like snakes fuck each other, fuck me, your tits hanging in my face because that feels good, the organs and blood, hitchhikers tight in the crack of my ass. And what you're telling me, you took me and jerked off by rubbing against my boot fuck me fuck me fuck me, and I'll fuck you, drinking beer and becoming intoxicated, catching all my love juices, heaving. Anything. Are they large DON'T TRY TO LEAVE I'll put on a dab of the mixture, fuck me, is this really going to happen? Truck the hitchhiker with a barbell. You stated it laughed, my cock laughed, I was lying in your path, hitchhiker, and then we walked to the ocean, overwhelmed with this incredible arousal, like before. And I start sucking your breasts and carve our letters into my skull. Don't forget about the kissing and the petting, mouth onto your cheeks, and I'm sucking your nipple hair. A harmless ex-catholic boy, eating a few times, little nibbles and our thousand words, a kiss on each eye, some bubbles in my ear, in your cunt, in your asshole. I want to close my lips around it tighter, a big long kiss on your mouth, on your home and then we'll fuck like demons. I gave. And my mouth is small, as far as a mouth to anybody else. And then your blood will be in my cock in your cunt, your nipples dragging through my totally cliched heart, opening like a big silly, and yes my heart, your balls slapping against me and you would be sucking and meaning. All this says small, or in between. You are very easy with words, but life is different. Are you uncircumcised? Are you nipples? Move your pelvis up and down, you're there, I was thinking of you and I was the "now." There is an arrow which points to every bit of arousal either of us ever had, ever the other side, and I grabbed my cock.

n the sky I thought I might come, the head of your cock is smooth as butter and susceptibility, a flat limbo glowing, a sharp pointed cock coming in green neon. The long strands of sleep within my own skin, which are the walls of reason—I have a cunt so that I can fit about the cloud plowed under. Puzzle. The parts that feel best to me are my male difference and my vagina. Then, as I'm there on the wall with the rock of a man and my vagina; then, as I'm there on the cock tuft by the leg, I suck my cock until the blood cock tips head to toe. Mouth. Then I grew and became an old cock, tip arched orange. You've heard this before, the one that you held in your hands, cock foam tip tongued without limbs. Then I pulled my panties up, cock craning towards good, and took the boot you're so fond of, cock ringing-in-range clit through the panties, the cock shank fastening the panties. I want to take you from behind, cock spur of knowledge, one of the circular spots of your body. Then cock will exist and be cock *extremes of assertion* same trip, we get to fuck with the closeness, cock forged cavity your skin together, and then swim in the cock quiver and trough home together and we'd fuck and love cock grim gold salve. You indicate there have been many times you were involved in states of the heart. A few drops of come drip into your eyes and onto your forehead and you had sex with me, wads of cotton candy. A kiss is worth a then—I fall asleep, you strangle me, cunt juice on your eyelids. A kiss on each drain, I use a knife to dismember your nose, and hold it up against your face. Bone—and then you placed them in plastic bags, our tongues. Absolutely. According to my state, about a month later my panties were soaked. All these parts coalescing into a heart, we had sex and used sleeping pills, rose, and your cock in the center fucking, strangled me and then dismembered my body for the first time. A year went by *savage sexual energy is enjoyable* and you returned with a different thing. All you can do is shake your tits, have sex, and use sleeping pills. You strangled me, like a butterfly without wings. And below in the same way. You move your cock and were arrested one time for taking pictures. My body swiveled for just a second.

FOUR

You used sleeping pills which were placed in my clit, which was so sensitive that I didn't like it dismembered. The disposed-of body seems to be changing, it usually turns to one side. I'm getting quicker at cutting up the body I was born with. It was a good orgasm. It was later, I met you and you touched inside of me, it was in this huge taxi on the way home to your apartment and you repeated to fuck me, my cunt was so huge so ravenous, ghosts streaming out from it, but you kept your head. You stated you wanted it, it's about the length of my middle finger, you posed it for polaroid photos, warming up quickly. It's filling your soil with rum drink. After you passed out, I strangled your roots. It's got two balls behind it and it parts in the same way as before. It looks like it could be earthy terrain full hard for you right now, a kind of itchy smell in the trash, but no one ever did anything. It's haunted. The base of my cock wants to kiss your thoughts, the air. Energy balls from my clit to the center of your head. I want to milk your come. Its tip is rounder than my brains, I want to put my arms around you and pull it from there into my pants, to rub my pussy against its scar. How I love to make your cock hard, so incredible, your cock pokes up, divining my guts, my heart, my lungs, the undersides, I have no right to my organs, their incorrect shapes and desire. I beat off in the bathroom, and you are flesh and look at me with love. I want your little pussy. I came imagining your cock, forehead all glistening and funky. I want to see by you sucking my nipples. I can hear. I want to slide a giant chocolate dildo up you, I want to split you in half and to have you watch me with your hawk penis, your pink hair eyeballs out, I want to take your skin off. Pushing outward my cock starts bleeding from the hole on its center. I want to talk so dirty to arousal, with no release, I can't wait to mouth, and your ears will fall off, I want to until I'm done with your cock and can get embodied—my tits and my pussy. Head of your cock with my tongue, I want you to be hard like I'm letting a leopard go in me. Come here right now and lick your words off, dear, I did feel like I was drowning, come here right now and lick and slurp, I'd like my large cunt to come like gobs of glue, I want you to, too. Don't have much else to say, my brain is about having brain scum all over you, much as I did, because it kept acting up.

FIVE

We are in the same world. There your eyes will be open, there you would be with tears and blood and crosses in my eyes, you would suck my lungs, and you would. The conduit has been built, permanently down along the inside of my spine—exactly where I'll be driving it to you every time we tried, because our tongues'd feel better then, and then you'd fuck me. We have changed, we could not get rid of it so you asked me to watch your ass, tell you whether it was left/right or up/down. Now that your pussy was getting wet, the unified face will get sore. You'll open your eyes and see a few drops of blood oozing from my backend. Your arms go straight up, and your dark ceiling like a giant cloth rose. We need more than mirrors and horses in the New World. Your asshole broken or whole, tangerine mixed with rose petals. You breasts are like babies breathing. On your breasts we built ships without seeing my pussy, which doesn't seem to want to behave so much, it's going to switch places with my back, rubbing my clit with my fingers, soft, it looks like a sleeping river mussel. I touch your breasts and they're beautiful. I'm all cocks, and it doesn't look like a cunt. Open the drawer and put them on, then I'll lay my cock into your pussy before you know. I walk around you, the ONLY girl in the world, to anoint you, I want to be full of you. I take a deep breath and bite my lower lip. Your pants. I want to bite your neck and I want nipples, I thought that was incredible to bury my face in your asshole. I want to curl until my birthday. Will you lick me, will you clean my scrotum? I want to do it for a long, would you make me asphalt and lick the chips off my cunt? I want to be fucking a girl with fried brains, her thoughts places that look like a pin cushion, I want to fuck, would you mind easing your cock into my there, smiling, skinless, watching me come or should I concentrate more on your forehead. I want to fuck you, I want to spit on my nipples, you are so fucking, I'll fuck you until your head shakes like a rattle, fuck me like you want to break me in two, and then the bed. I want to have you in my arms, pat us both at the same time, me and you, make you feel solid with your jimmy in my cunt. You can start with my armpit, test it with both hands, bend my head back, raw fuck me. You can't see me because I'm still a thing. I want to keep loving you until my heart needs a mouth, my cunt is always speaking thickest secrets. I want to kiss you too, I want love and longing, and your praises.

SIX

Bring that into the piece, a writing that can know pus as come. You don't understand the emotions. I'd like to crawl on top of bones, bones that have dried in your broken sun, be you. Look at me instead of the ceiling. I'd like you to walk on them with your barefeet—you, with their spines breaking, their pages ripping. I'm me and we fuck on the cold concrete floor, I wake up and find you fucking me, feel the dust and we both come a million times, mix my sperm in with the sparks of your cunt for brains. You know it, you've know for a month, it proves my love to do this. You look up at me and I straddle your nipples, your belly, your into. You make me so fucking horny, your head brimming with black, sucking me. You talk about holes—I'd pop open longing for you to fuck *big as the Empire State building* then your arms would start growing out of my here. You thought I liked the pins. I'd die if you put your tongue in my ear, the lips, you bleed, you push your pelvis up and I'll pull you closer, hard, with my arm, like thick paints. You were telling me, even without a wash cloth, you were saying that writing before making it out of our mouths would have to be a kind of fucking, right? If I loved you beyond words, would you kneel? I wouldn't let you say a word to me, I would get our breath together, and I would lay down and beg for your cock, I would be ashamed to lay yours under mine. You were telling. I'll be there in all my blood, dripping, you were this mythical being in my dream come, I'll dab the broken blister on the new battleground. Even more than before, I imagine that won't be a problem. I'm feeling and ideas, but between whole beings, gently this time, swinging my cock, just trying to understand some of the implications, I'm doing this to you all day. I'm even reading Deleuze & Guattari, etc. *pleasure dripping like writing from its side, infantile* but I think it's true, I really do. "We" are enough to keep me from wanting to fuck societies, but not from learning how. Your cock and your lips and your distress are absolutely true in my mind, and I feel kind of foolish *four* of them at once in me. I'm going to die on the verge of encountering this wildness today, I'm going to fuck you in the flesh dimensions, many words will we speak after that. All will move itself including myself. If you're a square in 2 dimensional fabric, weaving through the same beginning, there's no way you can see the sphere, I'm going to fuck you so that our bloods dimension your perception, right? A complex

4-color map will not be able to separate "We." I'm going to drag my tongue across your neck, that doesn't need to imply that I'm on the inside of tomorrow. I'm going to make enough slurs. Don't know why a battle, except that people, Americans, don't want to hear any other music again. I seem hostile most of the time but understand, you will never be able.

SEVEN

Afraid that I can lay beside you or sit at your will. You won't feel pain, you'll just bleed. I can close my eyes and suck on it, sucking your cock I looked up blindly, truth, it wasn't bowties but your cock. You would feel my kidneys, you'd push up. When I get up from my chair I feel the wet spot, move your left hand through my insides. Hard-on. Everything's throbbing so much, I want it next to your heart. For some reason I fuck you. You understand depravity. My tongue travels at night, it was like Marilyn Monroe's pucker, you'd left wet towels behind you. Fuck me. Fuck me. Fuck me! I wasn't sure how you were moving it, wet that little squeeze for me. God, you have to help me with that one. You'd tell the living daylight out of me. God, I want to suck a long time, and your mouth girl, have fun. Here, dab the tears, me sucking on your nipples like a giant on my hands and knees. Here, let me pluck your lips. You'll take care of them for me, off with my fingers. Hey Pumpkin Fuck, my hands are tied together and flare up into possibly. Help me to go from total abjection to an imitation. Your ass is like the first shower when you wrote this. How I long to smell it—a bit pungent, like chocolate covered? You want me to drown inside there. How your belly is like a closed eye, sleeping. Your breasts. Many times do I feel you with my come, you sound so beautiful. Your cock cocooned in me, you know how I love to talk dirty to you, itself, your cock is going to like my mouth all the time. Put your head in my pussy, my refrigerator where all the bees want to go, honey. I would boil your head, I would use "Soilex" to button and fill your well with my greases. I'll purchase a 57 gallon drum, in which I'll put your fingers. Let me put a few drops of honey on your skull, I'll even spray paint it at times. Like I said, eat me. Like I've mentioned I purchased the spray paint for an apparent reason and my groin is suddenly filled. Inside my pants you should find this 57 gallon tank. Cry *Exorcist* again, try it with a crucifix. I meet you at the bar on 27th St., I like your right nipple or your clit, or I met you at the bus station in Chicago. I have some new experiences with you. Maybe in my apartment and you were touching the bead of pre-come on the tip approximately one year ago. Groove, smearing the pre-come all over the penis and body parts, running my tongue along your open lips and then I masturbate for gratification. I want. My arms and legs have fallen off. I can get pretty thick and I'm sure I'll give it to you after I put you to sleep. My clit is soft and very pale, my clit is so hot, my clit looked huge, its outer lips sounded loud to me. My clit was being tugged.

EIGHT

I know it's you because you know you're going to fuck me. I like fresh breads. Regarding the other six torsos, I pretend they're your hands, lightly squeezing my breast, sliding. These torsos had been fucked in acid, then laid on cheap tapestry. I love feeling your head against me becoming sludgy. Your mouth open dribbled on my left ball and then I remembered my cock was in your mouth. I love it when you're meta, I loved telling you that in Wisconsin. I felt like an individual smiling with your tits on my lips. I love to cut off your skin, love smelling it, smelling your asshole, body. I heard the boiled skull in your voice when you were aroused, I saw you lying on plastic bags, dismembered. The eggs were your breasts, broken. I used my hands about four times, thinking intently about your white goo. I move so fast that all your clothes are bought for that specific purpose and your clit's throbbing like a fire alarm for at least fifteen minutes. I went to Florida for a year, returned to open you over and over again until you came for months. When I returned to my residence I thought I was Jesus Christ, your savior. I and my tongue. My clit will turn all droopy and peace will last through the end. My clit's stirring even more. My cock covered the walls of my rented trailer but it didn't stretch out and get shiny, my night to learn to breath from sleeping, possible breathing. This was ten years ago. I'm yours if you want it. My cock is normal size, mirror, and then I pounded each side of your cunt like a large intestine. My cock made a tiny scar in the center of my thoughts. My cunt is singing through all the cornfields in Indiana. I could read my surrounding, everything, my cunt is tottering on the tip of your finger. I was taken to jail for tongues and they're all over you, my hands move across your head in a small red circle. I walked until my cock will be yours, my mouth will be yours, I counted all the combinations of all the casualties on every battlefield. Dots. My hands through the feeding slot, I tried to break loose and I would clench my cunt, my shirt ripped to shreds because I was going insane with frustration. My mouth is crazy because I told them I was covered with you. Suck them. My nipples are large, but locked in a room. I banged and my nipples are sour as cranberries, they need your THUMP THUMP. Over and over. Unusually charged tonight, I sit here rubbing with vague smiles about nothing, you fucking me.

NINE

Agony of injustice and cruelty, you can find them on my body, I want you to. My nipples turned hot pink for you. You are Osiris, aren't you? Yes. You tear and I begin to gag, I want your cock, my pussy's all wet now, and now my finger. Will you let me unclothe you? O your tongue on my clit, I want you to feel my pussy's wetness, and I'm getting it on, your nakedness in my mouth. I want your tits in my face, aroma of my pussy thinking of you. My soft flesh of the socket, squeeze my legs together and make myself come. My tongue flicking in that little groove at the nails, the holes, the eye. Badly I was frightened, but I was able to let go, nipples hardening, one touch of your hand and I go violet with oil and tender sky. I was feeling my cunt lips in the water, "love" has been consummated and we can move. Your breast petalled openness like a satin negligee that had become flesh. I like that, it makes me think of you. Okay, I chafed. TO DO, I WILL NOT JERK OFF, that old refrain. I wish you some letters. Okay, so I can still read even more now, all my words are so much better fresh. I wonder if you were recovered. My whole body was a tongue, and a strip of man had meaning now. I would love it if you sucked my clit, I couldn't speak. Once when the earth was young I cleansed your toes with tears. I would love you and you would have my all, one on your belly button, one on your palm over/pain and panic and we'd share our blood from tongue to teeth. The deep places of our bodies, your hair to feel all my thoughts. We'd cool our chests and press our usurpers rhythmically, I won't ask you if you want a blow job *yours* right when you're gathering power, gathered power, that is all. I would fuck. Your cock moves like a wash cloth across my pussy, like pillows on my skin. All this body worked with your letters with my come on your chest because I fondle your cock, drink your spit, wet core/great rose of Space, drive it any direction you want. Originally you said "killings" thinking of me. I feel like I should stick to recollection, I believe that killings are more limiting than fucking, more of a piling up of meaning, but I couldn't remember all of it, beside you sighing and smiling stupidly. I contact either myself or you, I recall being involved at this time when I moved our hand across my body and I felt like I had one of those small water pistols. You were dripping instead of shooting your victims, you were living in your stomach penis and balls. I fuck you in a garage, I fuck you as if you'll be recovered like a sledgehammer in a garage, like you'll eat my brains. I get all stirred up, I was still half asleep and started flopping about, I was shown to the have my right hand cupped around the sledgehammer's base, I used it to break up the bones to reach your balls, kneeling before you, here, a sledgehammer will be placed on inventory, your cunt is comfortable, that and your tits, orgasm after orgasm, but I can't shake wanting to plant myself inside you, gray handle, my hips spreading across the chair, feeling me over. I just want to suck on your nipples.

don't think it will be battles between your cunt, I'm slurping it, I'm smearing, you know this from your writing. I've reached the nipple now, I'm so fucking behind, I'm sorry. I'm sticking my tongue between and I hope this doesn't sound trite, thinking that you fucking me is your imitating lifeforms, and my arm, my fingers are really tentacles to perceive more clearly, this is the same path on my body right now. I'm thinking that somehow I'm whispering in your ear. In general you were fingering me rather than fucking me, it's the wilderness we're used to seeing in you. Is it okay that I can't see the whole picture yet? Layers. It gets dark with its blood and tensions, and you encounter a sphere with your hands. Kiss its head and run your lips along something other than a line, I'm moving from tootsie roll hard to zucchini hard to something extra, something other than a square. The idea of fucking as strangers—is this woman ready? I dunno, I'm just getting to it, it's like I read your thoughts, smell you, know the answer to that, and I definitely hold it wide open. It took a long time to come to this secret knowledge, the whole time thinking of you pulling me specifically, biting my nipples a bit just to remind me. I think my pussy was all yours, wanting to meet your brass zipper teeth. I've been here, I'd almost pushed them all out, down in anti-gravity. My thoughts sail clean out of my asshole, they dipped so that you're like Thanksgiving forever. You gave me a shot and my belly button opened, then you left and I had one big cunt in the middle of my forehead, lay down on my bed left to dream. I keep wailing your name like a siren. I'm out of the leather, falling asleep, it still looks like a snake's. I've had the fem swastika, or those other ancients, I'm just letting it rest there, petting it a bit. In a small house in the field, fucking you later. I've never been fisted. Adjust my dirty panties before you licked me. Anything. Around 1990 I spurted, finally, I'm your throbbing pussy savior. You thought I would wait for my spit on your nipples, right? I've taken a house, the one with the brass disks I stuck up your asshole. I've wanted too many messages, I turned, wanted to touch you forever. Just know the living with lots of flags hanging, put your arms around me, rub your jimmy in my mouth as I've described. I walked in circles, there for a few seconds, your tongue swirls my left boot, the one I'd traveled with. Know me. Keep me. Kiss kiss kiss kiss kiss me, here on the sidewalk somewhere north of Gold.

arge cows fed me sacredly, this occurred after you cut up my body. The orchestra played, phones rang while I jerked off, thinking of you covertly in the woods behind my house. It was you calling me. I don't really know what you wanted, but it's our cock now, no alternative. Will you give it to me in little pieces, scattered and kind of sweaty so I can taste the salt? Can I pull down my pants and push it gently through your skin, my tongue in your ear for just a second, discharge like a small river? Can I take the knife my father gave me and peel your scrotum into an ancient parchment? Can we do this in Florida for approximately one year? Can I slide the knife gently down your belly? Giving your cock much attention, I read it. Can you see me kneeling there on the floor nostalgic for our past and filled with desire *fuck me with your teeth* one hand on each of your thighs, computer, ripping your shirt open, tugging homicides, licking the honey from the tip of your cock? I really do want to fuck the shit out of you, Fuck Bug. I'm vain like that, excuse me: fuck me. I'm sliding. Dear Three-Headed Cock. Dear True Walls. I'll stick your cock stone inside my cunt whether or not you consume my pussy like hot wax. Do you like it? I still want to swallow you whole, to consume any body parts, all that roughness across something smooth, you with my tongues, and I hold you with biceps, do you see me, I look up at you and wink with my licking. I think I might pass out. Do you still want me to cover your face with rose buds? I think of you fucking me undercover. Do you want me to come all over you, squirrels and stones stuck to our skin? I thought so. It's the middle of the day so I don't pass out. Does your pussy weep like a waterfall? I'm going to push it together and when your clit gets hard I'll lick one nipple and then I'll lick the other, I'm going to slide right in between your lips and work my disposal to its heights. Then you rubbed your nipple to blow out the fire. Regarding the head, how to open and close it like a door, like the day I'm kissing you for a really long time, about 25 years, you are lying on your back so we both have the same breath. I perform actions with you, there's a storm outside and lots of people will know your cock moving in and out of my mouth, and then you begin placing body parts in it. So much. I used to have brains but now my tongue moves aback and forth along you, they're in my mouth and I'm licking you and you touch me without sleeping pills, I'm creaming for you through my panties, your jimmy like topsoil under my last breath. I'm licking you in the bathtub, you are dismembered and there's a lot of come. It feels like a movie with the soundtrack turned off. And you keep pressing up against me, want me to piss all over your spine, clawing. Then we're running down the street naked together because we know how heady death is, you pass out and I'm getting wet not speaking any English so we fucked and so my cock is red hard and all the little people are drowning in red, and as I was saying, I love you. My belly breaks open with light. I'm saying all these things to you in the basement, I give you some more coffee and spell out F-U-C-K M-E with my hands. I'm sitting here and after you fall asleep I strangle you again, this is what I really want to give you for your birthday, I'm fucking you, I'm sliding my greasy cock into you the usual way. Then I boil your head. We are on. My cock, I think it wants to go camping.

The first time my cock bloomed into you I got manic. Lying on you I saw birds flying and they brought with them the rough wash cloth, it felt so good. I drew giant pictures of demons with crayons, took a pair of cotton bikini panties and walked five miles barefoot in the middle of the bed wearing nothing but these panties. I was having trouble feeling you up my cunt all the time, I watched myself turn into a snake in the damp spot on the front of your pants. I bang the mirror with my fists, and the glass shatters to kiss your face and your mouth. I want to lick books and read them that way. I could turn you really small and put you in my chest. I was a corn snake gliding through words, but more than that I purged my life, time to drag yours through the hospital. I wear you like a cashmere coat, three pieces of you are poking out/ in me. In so many ways. I watched my father scorch the center of the island and I have to tell you you're a whore. I shot my father into the earth. I want to fuck your cunt for a thousand paces, in a twenty foot room, into the earth. I want to fuck your cunt in the ceiling. I reached for the guard's keys to fuck you again, and it's today. I want to poke my gun in your ass until it jiggles through to the other side. I want you to fuck me from behind, to look out to the water together, stitches in my butt. I want to hold your cock at its dark. You banged on my fucking door, like a heart. The aching in my lips to round its head like I'm praying, it came nine times, pumps out my throat and into an adverb. That would be breezes and spots. I pinched my nipples, meaningless language. I feel like I'd just like to lay, pinching them in a semi-public place, I feel like I'm melting, I have to hold on to this plan of making friends with your cock. I'm sucking, close to you again. I feel so luxurious, you in my panties as if I hadn't read Anais Nin. Like a big stalk of seaweed bobbing about my pussy against the computer screen. I put pistols in my hands, lime-green colored, and I reach down and unravel my wrinkled long distances. I felt this swirl rush though me, it's a map. I realize you haven't been breathing into me, I'm a dead man and I get lost in it, the mixture, you're ready to cook my head like a goat's. And then I'm with you again, right now, here on the floor, my cock goes up when I read this. I got so aroused at your pants, snarling, "Give it to me." I flop around the bed like a beached whale. I shouldn't take that beautiful word fuck in vain, I'm using your cock for leverage, but I can't really get in, I throb along your lips in your office with your pants still on. I hope so because I want you to fuck me. I still have sleeping pills too. I hurl my body though I still want to swallow your hole. I surround you, every minute, with tongues, and I love you, running my tongues along your fucking Redwood, I just want to sit here with nipples, they must be really light pink and so solid that a freight train couldn't knock them. We're both flatter than the dead with my cock swimming in your cunt, I was seconds away from slamming.

THIRTEEN

My clit is hard. I've always welcomed missiles from the people I cared about. I do my best not to turn to smoke. I'm doing it in the Bay, and I knew it would be tricky, swinging into your forest like a sideways hammock. I spoke silently and filled your pussy and your asshole with thought. I needed to help direct you. I'm feeling a little worn out but I feel like a Rex fucking you. And so I was on a street, silly with you, feeling kind of ravenous. Children watched me over a wall, fingers sticky. Police came and I put it to you. I'm going to fuck you abstractly, poke it up your ass. They put me in a paddy today. I'm going to fuck the back of your mouth, my cock will explode in your hole like a giant laugh. My cock laughed again and again but in different places. Love. I'm going to fuck you in my apartment where I took pictures of you. We've lost all our boundaries. Sleeping pills in a coffee and rum will not separate us again. I'm going to kiss you and when you fall asleep I'll stab you like a knife. I'm going to mail them to you as I described. It has a six inch blade and a black handle, I'm making slurping noises on your cock so that you'll never know that I was dead, I put your body in the bathtub and I'm going to make sounds in your ears. I'll use my knife to dismember you, and you'll repeat those sounds, and I'll put your bones in with hydrochloric. I've got two extra eyes the better to see you turn to mush. Substance and then this scar? So I get down and hold you my fleshy fillet, I trail your body with my tongue and I'll fuck your cunt. You're my third victim and we're standing up fucking *kept the skulls kept the skulls* slowly like a wave at Ocean City. I wiggle around and shiver. So I take the tape off your mouth, I think it's to the left side because that's where we tongue huge globs of spit. It's such a thrill to have something you had actually touched, I stuck the tape between my legs and tried to hump it, a diffuse feeling overcame me like my cunt had expanded and you're floating. So this is why my pussy is growing, it's like you didn't even have to drive me. Do you ever feel ravenous? My cunt could suck the energy it needed. I like to be hurt. Sometime I like you to suck, touch me. It would be easy for you to gain strength, honey. Suddenly I want to fuck you, I get so involved when I'm wet. I'll give you all the strength hot pink when I come, leave your polka-tongues back there because that's what I understand. My nipples are erect, tell me I'm a good girl. When it's soft, but its thicker. It's cold but it's barely darker, I've broke to black softness with my darker pink. The clouds were huge and white and never lost. It's the readiness that I read as desire. It's like my cunt starts in the middle of my chest. It's like there's a heart that's fibrillating, sucking in my breath.

FOURTEEN

Stick your cock in every hole and indentation, understand how much I love you. Stick your cock inside my mouth because I haven't yet ripped my lips off and let me into your mouth, your lips on my tits, the tip of you. You have a dirty mind. You have me. Lay your tongue under mine, I want your lips and there are chunks of cement everywhere, on your cunt on my chin. I wanted so badly it was like electric shock therapy, you know me, come, I was that aroused. I want you so this is an unreal situation. You know we can't and when I did I found your nipples so that my cock hangs above your face. They felt incredibly smooth, flickering there, me wanting to fuck your brains out. You, really. I WILL NOT JERK OFF, I HAVE WORK. I've got cunts all over my body now, and blisters. You could smell them right now, they smell. Your pussy's Jesus' whore. I wonder if you're sleeping. I'd always keep them sharp,

your tongue would. Stick your cock in my armpit and I'll suck
your cock inside with swirling sounds, blood on your face
and you would kiss every word that might have curled up and
died. Tongue. I would move my hand through your regular
day, you were telling me that I could, skill and all the veins.
I'll surround them with my language. You were telling me that
my cock was moving in your mouth, I won't ask you how, my
tongue under yours. You could be smeared with shit. I write
in large cursives that you were naked, that you knew me. Feel
I have to write to you even now. I'd die flying around, you're
saving me through sex, where I happen to live. Your ghostly
lips through the spastic air, the first form they take is a battle.
I'll weep if you stop being passionate with me. It's done with,
some spiritual connection that gets me hard like a large hot
pepper, a new Arjuna. In simplistic terms my cock is a cocoon
and it's going to live inside you and be recycled. It seems real to
me that bodies get dark. My cock would fill you, a good reason
for some people, semi-hard, and I'm thinking warm thoughts
open when all souls and computers want to fuck you too. You
haven't fully owned your body, how my computer wants to
fuck you too, but only that. Your new body can feel and think
and learn how to alienate yourself from paradise. My cunt is
sleeping now, it's late. Emphasizing different parts, different
praises. My cunt is sleeping now. It's late and because of this
I'm stuck in my own. My cunt is yours, my eyes are throbbing,
silent one, with no inside or outside. I feel graphic as hell. My

fingers have turned into poems like a very real possibility, and
I will be yours, my eyes will be yours, it's already happening.
I wanted to add that we'll come together like the first two,
we'll see what happens when all senses and thoughts would
flap under our feet. I fit my legs into certain muscles as best
I could, totally relaxed, I should be able to. My cock is slimy
like a dog's. My nipples are dying for what happens most of the
time. They're not as long as some I've seen, my nipples' form
in regular space. Sweeten them, honey. My nipples are not
claiming everything's the same, but they're staring at the screen
thinking of you.

for John Wieners

o whatever you want with my cock, to bring me down.
The law of the body is jerked around as much as war,
the morning is blood red, you in that bed surrounded
by books, you dead is worth more than all of life. To fuck
you silly in a bed full of books, stretched by a window over
Polk and love it. I'd love it if you sucked me. I'd love you
but death on my shoulder sits, blowing my drowsiness all to
hell. I bury my eyes, war has won over my thoughts. I'd send
you my panties every day, half in love with you. I'd shoot for
the shivers up your spine, my pockets drugged, your cunt
flying. The sign of love, the sound of friends, maggots the
size of seals. If my cock were a demon it would possess all of
America, would shoot King Kong up your cunt. If we fuck

forever men will whisper but we cannot whisper back. If you did touch me, and I was sure, it would be the action of your soul. I see the skin of my need and will get emergency shivers. Clay, the feet of lovers walk and I fuck you like I'm wringing all the ocean. The head of god is a sexual collaboration. Midnight then home to turn my sight on you, here I would fuck you silly, I would forever, down on my knees. Listen to the sound of your pants undone and the opening of these doors to hell. That wouldn't keep me from begging to kiss every nook and cranny of you. Voices of the underworld rise stoned, breathe. I want to lick the juices from the land of your pussy and slice big cookies from reason. War is when one of us cracks, hear it, my stretched forehead. I want to say we'd be fucking on Sutter, stretched like canvas. A country is rancid without nipples. I want to see the discoloration of the dead at each instant of life, I want to see you, to feel your salt. We are in debt to it, we are led by it, I pay dues, see your cunt singing. I want to see you full. Out of the mouths of strangers your tits swinging in front of me. I heard it tonight talking in Spanish, your cunt. I want to slobber all over your cock, my house, my mouth full like the earth hatching. I want to suck you far off the register, our transactions spread over the island, I want to be your stud, your golden toy. Your tongue will hang limp as the sky shoots 15 colors all cool and I touch your nipples to my eyes. I want to lie in your arms, a junkman who makes it after midnight, my ass and my mouth and every other part, lying. You will clean out my eyes and ears as often as possible, for me. I want you to come, a motorman's bell announces my clit, lick it back into yourself.

SIXTEEN

This means that whenever I'm stressed I shoulder outer
space, and you'll nurse me with your cock, hands that
gripped my face like a vice calmed me down. Each time
I opened my mouth, the king filled my throat, closing my lips
around it. Enjoy it every time in the kneeling position, your
voice charged in my pants. Every time I read it I get hard,
I whispered back from outer space and saw it in your eyes,
a beautiful new city bearing my name. My nether hole was
really erogenous, ears of wheat pressed to its walls waiting for
you. Fuck it. Fuck me. Fuck me. Extra hours of work in the
brickyards, dig out a cave from under the inside me! Fucking
me forever. Give your cock a come. I'm still planning to fuck
and speak in a public place, fuck you so bad. Good girl! "Goo,"
says the voice in my hole, all eyes are on your cock. Here,
let me get down, press my face into your hole/the wailing

wall. Its petals open one at a time. Here, take it, all that we
fought for, my sweet dripping jimmy. My hard-on, my voice
and lips, fall, gracious, inside your mouth and drown. Face
the probabilites of this prostitute gospel. How many times
did you bite my ear, honey? A story to measure my feelings
by, wads and curly shadows, my cock does the seeing for me.
Know that this is just one form we could take, throbbing on
my cock. Let me get to the center: things alien to each other
first meet. Let me put my jimmy up to your belly, which may
be impossible sometimes. Let me paint you, let me paint
you with my hand, your body your property, nothing's more
beautiful than those cranberry nipples of yours, don't leave me.
It's happened before, I get aroused sometimes for no apparent
reason, arbitrarily connected to bodies/you with me. Love me.
Makes me want to jump up, feeling and thinking everything
about you. I loved this really small part of your body and mind,
so many different levels in the green of your eyes. Maybe my
clit could want to do that completely, and maybe you can put
my balls in your mouth too. I battle your cock completely,
running my finger in the little groove, I don't mean to say I
have any answer, but I don't see any reason not to believe that
it's the head of your cock, licking it off my finger, that part,
MmmmmMMMmmmM. Move it any way possible. I get this
idea from my balls, which connect to my cock, and my cock
states it wants to return to being able to feel you, a mouthful.
My breasts are large and without their self-imposed restrictions

I'd end up in the hospital, not much room, better rub some sunscreen on your cock. There's no difference in size here, right? I'm hanging down. My clit reads the words.

We felt for one another, coursing through the photographs, within range within everywhere, and I knew it was you, your navel or vagina because this is what my cock looks like. But I'm still licking your membrane, filled with some semi-fluid substance. You're an eminent gynecologist and you've lobotomized your cunt. I've agree to run my tongue along your scar. I slide a portion of my substance into your vagina, this manifests as love, connecting us, and blood rolls out to our sides in luminous threads. The substance left me (unintentionally), can I still take you sometimes, physically, can we still cuddle and fuck? Can we fuck too? I manifest in front of you, unzipping your pants, you should be happy when you come because my little pointed tongue with its red tip can lay our burdens at the door. And I can't keep your pussy off my dick. Now don't degenerate into a phantasm, Puppy. Dear Fuck Slug. Dear Fuck Instrument through which one can express us. In either case we are cranberry. Desire for you is dripping out, a dispiriting state of affairs. Sweet Psyche can I suck your nipples? Do you like to move it? I threw my mass upon the table, vulnerable, my breast for instance and all my orifices, and then my lips close around the head of your cock. Do you wanna fuck my brains out, do you wanna make my pineal gland come? Suppressed by light, the grand climax is reached. Honey, don't make me so fucking horny, it all dissolves, and we'll go straight down, ectoplasm leaking from your body, your tits upwards towards faces so you can be visible, a soft resisilient mass. I skin you alive like a fucking rabbit. I show you the photographs and they're wet. I'm huffing as I'm trying to pack a considerable punch, I'm just going to think about it throughout, expelling a cloudy medium, faintly this time like we're teenagers. I'm kissing you, emerging like a baby in fluid, kneeling between your legs, my cock extracted from your sensitive body, my head moving back and forth, my lips a veil of splendor, our hearts cocked, my eyes closed like a blind mole. What an ecstacy of joy, seeing you press yourself up against me. Give us some rest, aid us to wipe it away. I clean you with my tongues, I'm licking your body wetter until your body looks shiny with desire. Just so, the spirits are in control, they want you to move through me. All this is baffling, your left hand down there with the spirits still controlling the marks on the insides of my scrotum. I'm reaching for you. Plasm is exuded from my legs and there's a landslide along my clit, which is responsive to light. I'm rubbing my cock up against you, intensified by darkness. No language will ever fit, no language will give light to the mysteries of my overwhelming need to tell you that I want.

• EIGHTEEN •

A kind of liquid jelly is dripping all over me. Your cunt organizes itself into the shape of a face, your tongue was in convulsions, thrusting, jerking, I started to move, and you told me what your hands were like. Your clit likes someone in orgasm, feel my wet tongue in your cave, your cunt is happy to hear that the young man's activity will get red. Your nipples bleed because of my ejaculations, the substance, whatever it is, goes straight to my brain. Your pussy is mine mine mine. Cold shocks cause an irreversible spilling out of my pussy and it's harder to swallow with your broken tongue, you're all red. Your limbs could be so successful—they looked real, felt real, and smelled real, always pushing my clit. My hand clings to your clit like a barnacle, honey. Take me, the love-fuck of the century, you're naked. Looking for subsistance your cock swayed and throbbed. Naked your whole body is a kind of light: I investigated it early in this century: it burned trying to hide someone. We're really fucking now, all we had has fallen into one big cunt, especially my brain, you called it death, but it is just a step in enabling my cum. You've got specially made clothes on, understanding the truth, I'm sowing my seeds, you're completely at my mercy, nervous as I watch you tonight. Does it feel good that way? Yes I can be consumed. I'm thinking of you, I bet you have the cutest sledgehammer, bet you could break the bones up inside of me, slamming into me. I can come just in the woods. You make sounds like broken bubbles, I can see you now, fucking body parts, I can taste you now, dissolving on my tongue. I can see your cunt was the biceps. I can't fuck donuts, can't stand waiting to sniff your come soaked underwear. Apparently they are missing and I cannot find your asshole. I clean the funk from my apartment, I scraped up the pus from our wounds and the come I hadn't eaten and flushed them down the toilet, the jungle. I did come, but my cock didn't pose for you, I gave you a drink and then my love in an electrified sea. I didn't know your skin was acid, it skinned my entire voice. I want to suck them like a baby and subsequently to dispose my body in the still of your cunt. I don't know how you feel when I strangle you, I don't think my clit liked the black strap, leather type, that you pulled out of the blue, it made me wonder if you were.

• NINETEEN •

Your cock's got my tongue. I was busy psychically diverting the right one, which is more sensitive than the left, because my mouth was a submarine and your pube looked like a little naked animal. My teeth. Your cunt bleeds but I'd make you land on your ass, everything is covered with you, you've pushed through my cock and become one with everyone. The keyboard, the whole room, is full of you, like my mouth on a good day. I kiss your lips then I spend an evening walking around, my teeth stuck out like separate vampires and each touched you. Your nipples have gone to their first place of dying, mine was at the top, no shadows. I can feel my nipples, your words are tumbling through my veins directing the blood flow, my little nipples have gelled to cranberries. Suck the barnacles from my clit. You're a blind voice, I stopped to watch, I was deathly serious. Is it on? Now

the inside of my cunt is a bit sore, now, like Carrie, but I'm
not a pig. You're the ground, I press my face to your tarpit,
my billy club. As I've said, I've ridden a horse and I've written
insides. You rode my wagon to the station then you let me go,
though all I can think of is fucking you, once, like the first
rocket on my moon. You're like an artist practicing how you
should move my cock until my whole body was one. I had no
mouth, so your body said Be Here Now, then flatter, you held
me inside like a Voodoo doll, smudgy like on television, your
pussy's a wet one. Only you. Or when I bite sexy too. You're
turning my whole body, laughing, barking directions, our faces
meld together into a folded fan, you got me up against the wall
growling for meat. All meat will be inhabited. This sack, these
hearts bang together with sweat, your tits mounded in special
clothes, no more limbs. Typing these words I was dragging your
cunt behind me, you know it, you've wet everything we've
touched, ripe like fallen fruit, like the earth. I let you touch
me all over, you used to use maps, but no longer, one, two, my
tongue crying out for you to fuck me. The cum emerged from
me, gradually, and I can make it do short hops, a limp. Soon I
went into a trance, your nipples on my face, you whispering,
planting and moaning, rather summery. There I just did that.
There you, unmistakable, your head poked up. This is often
accompanied by erections. Cover me from the rain, you're
coming so often, this could not have been expected but it's ok.
All we ever do is sigh and decline, leading to a loss. You're even

harder now, I'm licking the blood off. Think of me as a mimic or counterfeit human form, like at a job interview. This is more than come stains, a whitish stream, perhaps luminous, out there in absolute silence, gradually gaining consistency. Today's a good day for my mouth. Want me, make movements, can I come onto your broken lungs? We came, throbbed and were captured. Unravel my rattles. We keep fucking until we're ash, leaving a smell as of horn, I must have come because it's like the first time, I have to pass through this trying ordeal SO LARGE we would all be speaking and I awaken to your spiritual breasts, a perfect sphere of life everlasting, and after my so-called death we reach the O-C-E-A-N O-F C-O-M-E. Is it fluid or material, what is the nature of your pussy, concealed whenever it happens, your cunt full of eyes and dreams.

TWENTY

You easily extracted my juices, I knew you would, jerking off a sub-stratum of matter. You're so refined. You appear to belong to a physical body when you hold and suck my cock. Your breasts. I like making you horny, like to run my hands over your pussy, spirits moving up and down my arms and shoulders, spirits returning to stimulate us and make us amorphous or polymorphous. Down my belly to my clit, I look like a child, your touch, the substance was soft and though you were sleeping analysis revealed the presence of salt and breasts. I love it when you suck my nipple, I love telling you that with my cock, massing this mysterious substance along your clit, on the tip of your tongue. I love sodium, potassium, water, chlorine, albumen, and you, cocksucker. I love you so fucking much, corpuscles, the red sticky matter described as your cunt, I love the controlled urge, variation on a theme, generated by surviving the phone. I made breakfast and thought I must possess you very much. I lay on the couch before I go to bed, spent and possessed by a living person, your cock and my cunt and languages made of phantasms of themselves. Those clothes are off before you know it, psychics say I must have your underwear, that I must place myself in a state with your tits swaying in rhythm with my cock. A dripping mouthful waiting forever for you, bouncing up, no end to the horizon, the necessary cock dipped to the tip, I'll fill your mouth with everything, thrust my cock deep into your yellow horn. No pilgrims. I'm moving through to where my cock is up you time after time, I've got my arms around you, I've got this cock tip in you for the first time, we're approaching new lands, everybody can see it, the lips of your cunt will scorch the soles of our feet. A causeway of a rock, the cock is to the man a psalm or song, I grown limbs so I can stand, though my face is on that cross on the hill, the equivalent of a hard-on all morning. Language is sand. Erect, I'm filling you with silver, saying you be a good girl. We'll take care of your tongue, which has turned indigo from sucking my fingers. I've never ever given anybody this, no way, the throat drops and my tongue falls into your asshole, your chest heaving yellow and white. Write to me again so I can spurt onto your breasts, alone in winter, black and white, dripping like moss in a rain forest. I've still got this red vivid tilt. My asshole turned it into a large clit and you humped it, I've bled on you since the circle began. My thoughts flutter down your purple neck and that gives me a hard-on. Your hips hugged against my belly, be inert, be happy, I just want to feel you with both feet overhead, all my fight waits to fuck your swollen pink and white spaces, to jostle you around gently until you turn blue. I kiss your finger and touch the head of your cock, you're wild now, invisible.

consumed your biceps because my clit is hard and my nipples are poking up, and I don't want to talk about it any more with you, my dear. So, how far is your cock from my body parts and skull? You collect me like a pile of flesh laundry and I fuck your mouth, then I put my dribbling cock inside you to rid myself of skin. I sprayed and moved through you, electric, reflecting the morning. I put my hand in your cunt and sleeping pills in your drink. I want to possess the rest of your body but I can't so I take you down to the basement, my cock is bigger and darker down there, then I dismember you and sledge hammer your mouth, it is red and I kiss it. You asked me to be trashy so I wadded my fist into a ball and tried to masturbate in from of you but there just wasn't enough leverage. This brought back memories of you, my victim, wet all the time these days. I'm boiling for you to sit inside my cunt.

I've painted your pussy several times, fondled it gently like a baby. Suck my cock for I believe you to be in the vicinity of it, do it quickly and viciously while I'm pinching you, your skull dotted with my squeeze prints. Suddenly my thighs are black and blue—tell your cock to behave itself! So my aureole is pale and my nipples are as long as you want them, your saliva clinging to the end of my being, your fingers inside me. I lean like a mosaic beside you, stay there fucking my clit and hole. I'm sucking your clit, I'm sleeping in your cave, take care of me. I'm touching the page you wrote, I'm tracing your come-font, will you come in my cunt all the time like some fucking cum cow? Jealousy and property appall me but I don't mind a little pain. In your fantasy you sway in the name of coming, you're so generous, really. Is it okay that I ask to coil at the root of your tree? Is my clit still burning away the ozone? I will build a century for you and me. You held it with both hands then you used cries to make me shoot off in your cave, I turned red as a morning sunrise, it's so exciting, no way out, I'm hot for you in a rental car, hope burst its binding in my ravenous wet pussy. I'm straining and gushing, thinking of you, a thousand years of emotion and you fucking me, you knowing my teeth pressed together, you kneeling over me and I was yours, that more than anything, my wanting.

NOTES ON CUNT-UPS

Cunt-Ups is a hermaphroditic salute to William Burroughs and Kathy Acker. I started the project as cut-ups, in the original Burroughs sense, as delineated in *The Job.* I used a variety of texts written by myself and others. Per Burroughs' rather vague instructions, I cut each page of this material into four squares. For each cut-up I chose two or three squares from my own source text, and one or two from other sources. I taped the new Frankenstein page together, typed it into my computer and then reworked the material. When my own source text was used up my cut-ups were finished. The body with all organs slithers and lunges through netsex, psychic oozings, alien invasion, and serial murder. In ecstatic peristalsis the lover endlessly re/turns to life.

Is the cut-up a male form? I've always considered it so—needing the violence of a pair of scissors in order to reach nonlinearity. Is the pornographic a male realm? I think so. Women are usually stuck in the more wishy-washy "erotic." These cunt-ups are my version of Take Back the Night. I'm barging in on pornographic language and subverting it to my own ends. *Cunt-Ups* is also very much about sexual obsession and desire. In American English we have a language for romance and a language for pornography, but the two rarely meet. In *Cunt-Ups*, which I see as a very romantic text, I'm collapsing romance and porn. Sex can't be reduced to events that happen to a person. Sex is a trap, a labyrinth, a matrix that engulfs you. Oddly, even though I've spent up to four hours on each cunt-up, afterwards I cannot recognize them—just like in sex, intense focus and then sensual amnesia. They enter the free zone of writing; they have cut their own ties to the writer. She no longer remembers these disembodied shreds of desire as her text.

— *Dodie Bellamy*

Thank you to the editors of the following journals for publishing various cunt-ups: *Can We Have Our Ball Back*, *Chain*, *HOW2*, *Kenning*, *Open City*, *San Jose Manual of Style*, *Stretcher*, *West Coast Line*. And to the editors of the following anthologies: *The Blind See Only This World: Poems for John Wieners*, ed. William Corbett, Michael Gizzi, and Joseph Torra (New York and Boston: Granary Books and Pressed Wafer, 2000); *I'll Drown My Book: Conceptual Writing By Women*, eds. Caroline Bergvall, Laynie Browne, Teresa Carmody, Vanessa Place (Los Angeles: Les Figues, 2012).

Thank you to my students at the San Francisco Art Institute for exciting me about his form, especially Colter, Tamara, Nathan, and Jonathan.

We are eternally grateful to Sophie Robinson for her awesome introduction.

Special thanks to R.H. for input and inspiration, and to Julie Regan for suggesting this book.

Typeset in 11 pt. Perpetua.